# UP CLOSE

# FUR & FEATHERS

## A CLOSE-UP PHOTOGRAPHIC LOOK INSIDE YOUR WORLD

Written by Heidi Fiedler

Quarto is the authority on a wide range of topics.
Quarto educates, entertains, and enriches the lives of our readers—
enthusiasts and lovers of hands-on living.
www.quartoknows.com

Written and edited by Heidi Fiedler

Photograph on page 20 by Ingo Arndt. Photograph on page 23 by David M. Phillips / Science Source.
Photograph on pages 24–25 by Pedro Jarque Krebs. Photographs on pages 26 and 50 by Brad Wilson.
Photograph on page 40 by Igor Siwanowicz. Photograph on page 55 by Eye of Science / Science Source.
Cover photography and all other images © Shutterstock.

6 Orchard Road, Suite 100
Lake Forest, CA 92630
quartoknows.com
Visit our blogs at quartoknows.com

MIX
Paper from responsible sources
FSC
www.fsc.org
FSC® C104723

Printed in China
1 3 5 7 9 10 8 6 4 2

# Are You Ready for Your Close-up?

Look!
Closer…Closer…Closer…
Can you feel your brain tickling? That's the magic of looking at something way UP CLOSE. It can transform the ordinary into something new and strange, and inspires everyone from hi-tech shutterbugs to supersmart scientists to look again. So let's turn the ZOOM up to eleven and discover a whole new way of seeing the world.

# How Eye See the World

"Whatcha lookin' at?" That's the question people have been asking each other for thousands of years. The first humans observed interesting—and important—things like woolly mammoths, lightning, and each other. Early artists moved on to painting and drawing what they saw. Finally, in 1826, photography allowed people to capture what they saw in new and amazing ways.

Today, photographs are everywhere. Cereal boxes, bulletin boards, and T-shirts are all home to photos. A simple image search online can produce adorable images of bright-eyed babies or stark, white, snowy landscapes. Photographers capture everything from moments of joy and pain to the wonders that exist in the cracks and hidden layers of our busy world. They focus their attention on a huge range of subjects, and the images they produce reveal how everyone sees the world in their own unique way.

## The History of Photography

**Black & White Photography**

| 1826 | 1839 | 1859 | 1877 |
|------|------|------|------|
| Nicéphore Niépce creates the first photograph. It takes 8 hours. | Daguerreotypes capture rough images. | Photography goes panoramic. | Eadweard Muybridge invents a way to shoot objects—like horses—in motion. |

**Color Photography**

**1888**
Kodak™ produces the first mass-produced camera.

**1912**
The 35mm camera takes center stage.

**1930**
Flash bulbs help photographers capture images in low light.

**1935**
New techniques make color photography shine.

**1939**
An electron microscope reveals what a virus looks like.

**1946**
Zoomar produces the zoom lens.

**Digital Photography**

**1976**
Canon® produces the first camera with a microprocessor.

"**Photography**...has **little** to do with the things you **see** and **everything** to do with the **way** you **see** them." –Elliott Erwitt

**1992**
The first JPEG is produced.

**2015**
Instagram is home to over 20 billion images.

# Extreme Close-up!

Photography has been helping people express how they see the world for nearly 200 years, and in that time, things have gone way beyond taking a simple shot of a horse or a sunset. Today, photographers are pushing the limits of technology.

**Macro photographers** use large lenses to get WAY up close to their subjects. They can magnify an object up to five times its size, with special lenses that reveal patterns and textures that wow viewers.

**Micro photography** goes even farther. It uses a microscope to reveal details humans could never see before. It can make a blood cell look like a glowing planet or a priceless jewel.

With textures that beg to be touched and curious faces, birds and mammals are favorite subjects for photographers. Some shutterbugs are scientists studying the surface of a hummingbird's tongue in intense detail. Others are enthusiasts obsessed with capturing every hair on a cat's head. Together, their images help us see the natural world in a whole new way. Take a look!

# Getting the Shot

Photographers choose where and how they want to work based on what type of images they want to produce.

## Out in the Field

Macro photographers can take their giant lenses outside to capture animals in their natural environment.

## In the Studio

Working inside lets photographers have more control over the lighting, the angle of the camera, and their subjects.

## Under the Microscope

A microscope allows photographers to look at anatomy, such as feathers, in even more detail.

# The Masked Monkey

Mandrills use color, scent, loud screams, deep grunts, and body language to communicate with each other. Learning their language can be tricky for humans. When they bare their long teeth, they may be saying hello to friends—or warning someone to stay away. But the meaning of their famous colors is clear. They say, "Notice me!"

## Changing Colors

Young mandrills are born with dark fur and a pink face. As females grow, they stay dull and small. Adult males gain their bright face and rump when they are about nine years old and ready to attract the ladies. Their colors get flashier when they're excited, but they can fade if they lose status with the other monkeys.

**Scientific Name:**
 Mandrillus sphinx
**Size:** Up to 3 feet long
**Habitat:** Rain forests of equatorial Africa
**Diet:** Fruit, roots, insects, and small reptiles and amphibians

Mandrills usually live in **troops** with one **male**, several **females**, and their **young**, but they can form **groups** of **hundreds** or even **thousands** of monkeys.

# Feathered Fiesta

A flock of peacocks is known as a party—and what a pretty party it is! Like hummingbirds and butterflies, peacocks have feathers with microscopic, crystal-shaped pieces that reflect light to create fluorescent colors. But unlike many birds, peacocks can shake their tail feathers. The "eyes" stay still while the rest of the feathers shake, rattle, and show off. Males with the longest, heaviest feathers shake them fastest. Whatever their size, the result is mesmerizing.

## Heavenly Colors

Hindus celebrate peacocks as sacred birds. They believe the blue, gold, and red spots on the feathers symbolize the mystical eyes of the gods.

**Scientific Name:** Pavo cristatus
**Size:** 30 to 50 inches
**Habitat:** Forests and rain forests in Asia and Africa
**Diet:** Plants, insects, and small animals

Peacocks are **males**. Peahens are **females**, and **babies** are known as "peachicks." **Only** males have **dramatic trains**.

# A Hypnotic Hunter

The Great Gray Owl's powerful eyes lie at the center of spellbinding rings of feathers. Shaped like tunnels, rather than simply spheres, their eyes can absorb extra light, giving them intense night vision. Their large flat faces cast the sound of nearby prey into their ears. One ear is higher than the other, helping them decipher if the sound came from above or below. Special veins and arteries in the neck allow owls to swivel their heads at an otherworldly angle. Sharp talons seal the deal when they plunge after prey.

**Scientific Name:** Strix nebulosa
**Size:** 24 to 33 inches
**Habitat:** Forests of North America, Europe, and Asia
**Diet:** Small mammals

## Lunch Meat
After a meal, owls regurgitate a dry, compact pellet. Pull it apart, and you'll find the undigested fur, feathers, bones, teeth, and claws of their prey. Scientists dissect the leftovers to learn what owls are feeding on.

Although it is **one** of the **largest** owls, the **Great Gray** is **mostly** made of **feathers.**

# Phenomenal Flight Patterns

With their rainbow feathers, hummingbirds have inspired some fancy names, including *fairy*, *wood star*, and *sungem*. They may look delicate, but wind and rain aren't problems for these fierce fliers. They're almost pure muscle, and their wings allow them to fly up, down, sideways, and backward. They can even hover! Hummingbirds flap their wings in a rapid figure-8 pattern, which produces the buzzing sound we often hear before we see these beauties.

**Smart** hummingbirds **scare** off **predators** by **building** their **nests** close to **hawk** nests.

**Scientific Name:**
Calypte anna
**Size:** Under 4 inches tall
**Habitat:** Western North America
**Diet:** Nectar and insects

## Must. Have. Sugar.

Flying at top speeds burns a LOT of calories! Long, slender beaks let hummingbirds collect nectar created deep inside flowers. They drink 3 to 7 calories a day, which might not sound like much, but if they were human size, they would need to drink about 155,000 calories each day!

# Night Stalker

The leopard's powerful roar sends shivers through the jungle. This predator is ready to pounce—and prey know it. Leopards are comfortable on land, in trees, and in the water where they can feast on fish. These big cats are nocturnal and prefer to hunt alone at night. If you spot one lounging in the trees, it might be protecting its kill. Leopards often drag the body of their prey up in trees for safekeeping.

## Spot the Difference

Can you tell the difference between the fur on these big cats?

Leopards have lots of flower-shaped spots called rosettes.

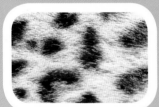

Cheetahs have solid, smaller, more even spots.

Jaguars' rosettes have thick outlines around them and are larger.

**Scientific Name:** Panthera pardus
**Size:** Over 6 feet long with tail
**Habitat:** Across Africa and Asia
**Diet:** Rodents, antelope, pigs, and baboons

**Brave** enough to **pet** a **leopard?** It might **purr**—although the **sounds** it makes will be closer to those made by a **motorcycle** than a **kitten.**

# The Sonic Boom

Approaching this bird, you may first hear a hiss and then a whistle warning you away. But when you feel a rumbling bass note so low and powerful that it shakes your bones, you'll have no doubt: This is a cassowary. The cassowary is known as the most dangerous bird in the world. Its powerful legs propel it forward at high speeds, and it can jump nearly 7 feet in the air. If this bird can't escape or scare away predators, it will use its 4-inch-long claws to slice them open. Cassowary? Casso*wham*!

**Scientific Name:** Casuarius
**Size:** 4 to 6 feet
**Habitat:** Tropical forests and wetlands in Australia and other islands
**Diet:** Fruit and seeds

Cassowary **fathers** take the **lead** in **caring** for **chicks, incubating** eggs and **teaching** them **how** to **find** food.

## Secrets of the Cassowaries

Despite their showy appearance, these birds are notoriously difficult to study in the wild, and there's much we don't understand about cassowaries. Some native people celebrate them as a primal goddess. Scientists wonder if the casques, or helmets on their heads, help them communicate. And what about the colors of their wattles? Do they reveal their moods? We don't know—yet!

# A Fierce Feast

Huckleberry. Buffalo berry. Twinberry. Serviceberry. This bear's diet is *berry* full. Of course, grizzlies also love salmon, and they're not above stalking elk and moose. During the summer months, bears gorge on 50,000 calories a day. Feasting in the forest helps these super hibernators pack on the pounds they need to sleep through long winters and fast up to seven months. *Mmmzzzzz....*

**Scientific Name:** Ursus arctos
**Size:** 5 to 8 feet
**Habitat:** North America, Europe, and Asia
**Diet:** Berries and anything else they can find

A **hump** of **muscles** in the **grizzly's** back gives the bear **extra strength** for **digging**.

## Grizzly Graffiti

Grizzly bears mark their territory in the forest by rubbing the trunks of large trees, biting off pieces of wood, and scratching bark. The meaning of their marks is clear: I was here!

# Cockle Doodle Boo!

Polish chickens are famous for their dramatic bouffants. But despite their wild appearance, these quirky characters are usually calm and happy as long as their feathers don't droop into their eyes. But cover their peepers, and these chicks will get spooked!

**Scientific Name:** Gallus gallus domesticus
**Size:** Up to 25 inches tall
**Habitat:** Farmlands
**Diet:** Grains, seeds, fruits, vegetables, and grass

## Focus on Feathers

Scientists use scanning electron microscopes (SEMs) to get closer to their subjects. The work is done inside a vacuum to keep the process clean. Subjects, like this feather, are often stained or dipped in metal. To create an image, the SEM hits the subject with electrons and records how it bounces back. Then photographers add colors like hot pink to make the details easier to see.

**Chickens** began **living** on human **farms 10,000** years ago. **Today** there's even a **nail polish** that **tastes** just like fried **chicken**!

# A Mysterious Mirror

# Breaking Z Code

What secrets lie between the black-and-white lines that cover a zebra's back? The answer is one of nature's mysteries. Every zebra is covered in a unique pattern. Scientists use a program called StripeSpotter to scan and sort zebra photographs. Some scientists think the stripes work like an optical illusion that hides zebras from predators. Others think the stripes provide protection from the sun. Or maybe the patterns help zebras recognize other zebras. Zee answer is an enigma!

## The Z Team

Zebras are always on alert for predators. They often team up with wildebeests and giraffes to look for danger. If a zebra is wounded, the others in the herd will circle around it until the danger has passed.

**Scientific Name:** Equus quagga
**Size:** Up to 5 feet tall at the shoulder
**Habitat:** Savannas, grasslands, and woodlands of Africa
**Diet:** Grass and other plants

**Zebras** sleep **standing** up. That's **one** way to **get** your **ZZZs**.

# Gliding Through Life

Like many birds, male mandarin ducks are more colorful than females. They use their bright feathers to attract a mate. But once ducklings have hatched, males molt. They shed their wing feathers and lose the ability to fly. Their new look may be drab, but they sacrifice fashion for camouflage. Their dull feathers help them hide from predators. When it's time to mate again, their true colors come alive once more.

**Scientific Name:** Aix galericulata
**Size:** Up to 19 inches long
**Habitat:** Lakes, ponds, and streams in forests of Asia and Europe
**Diet:** Seeds, grains, and water plants

## A Happy Couple

Mandarin ducks choose their mates carefully and stay with them for many seasons. In China and Japan, they are admired for their close relationships and celebrated as a symbol of happy marriages.

Just **24 hours** after being **born**, mandarin **ducklings** must **jump** over **15** feet **down** from their **treetop** nests to the **ground**.

# Aliens Among Us

Elephant? Piggie? Cow? Nope. And knowing that a group of them is called a candle isn't any help. So what is this strange creature? Tapirs are stubby cousins of the horse and rhinoceros, and they love to play in the water like hippos. Their hoofed feet help them walk easily through mud. Like elephants, they use their trunks to grab a bite to eat. They even use them to snorkel when they swim!

**Scientific Name:** Tapirus
**Size:** 4 to 8 feet long
**Habitat:** Tropical forests in Southeast Asia and Central and South America
**Diet:** Fruit, berries, and leaves

## Creatures of Habit

Once tapirs find a watering hole they like, they travel there every day, using the same route. At night, their footsteps create deep ruts in the ground, and their movement clears the leaves from trees. In the morning, a tapir tunnel can be seen in the forest!

**Tapirs** can often be **heard** making a **high-pitched whistle** that **sounds** like a **car screeching** to a **halt.**

# A Wink of Pink?

# The Prettiest Parade

Left, right, left! Squawk, honk, squawk! Flamingos march to the beat of their own hot-pink drum. Flocks of thousands can often be seen preening, but their most impressive display happens when they move into formation. Together, they march in unison, as though an invisible leader is steering them. Ten-hut! These birds deserve a salute.

**Scientific Name:**
  Phoenicopteridae
**Size:** 2 to 5 feet tall
**Habitat:** Shallow lakes around the world
**Diet:** Algae, shrimp, and other small crustaceans

## You Are What You Eat

Flamingos thrive in salty lakes that other birds avoid. Their long legs help them wade into deep water, where they eat shrimp and other pink morsels. Their bright color comes from the pink pigment in their food.

Flamingos have **fascinated** people for **thousands** of **years**. **Spain** is **home** to a cave **painting** of a **flamingo** that's over **7,000** years **old**!

# African Royalty

Legend has it, these cranes received their crown after coming to the rescue of a great African chief. He was so grateful for their help that he ordered the court magician to make every crane a crown of gold feathers. Today the effect is aristocratic, but also savvy. The headdress helps the crane blend in with the tall grasses that grow where it lives. Bow down, peasants. Bow down.

**Scientific Name:** Balearica regulorum
**Size:** 4 feet tall
**Habitat:** Near rivers in Africa
**Diet:** Plants, insects, and other small animals

Many **believe seeing** a **crowned crane** is good **luck!**

## At the Crowned Ball

During breeding season, crowned cranes dance to attract mates. Popular moves include swaying, wing lifting, and jumping high. Best of all, they know how to make a royal entrance: Their mating call sounds just like a bugle.

# Wild Style

Top knots. Side-swept bangs. Shaggy layers that go on for days. Mammals are the only animals that have hair, and they can rock everything from a fuzzy buzz cut to a spiked mohawk. Many mammals have an undercoat of short ground hair with longer hair on top. The ground hair keeps the animals warm. The top layer helps their skin stay dry. Fur also helps mammals hide from predators—and look fashionable doing it.

**Rural Elegance**

**Cute Curlicues**

**Drama Queen**

**Shabby Chic**

**Wispy Whiskers**

**Blown Away**

# Gobbledygook

The turkey was first domesticated in Mexico thousands of years ago. It was brought to Europe in the 16th century, and its name reflects its worldly history. In America, females are called hens, while males are known as gobblers. Ancient Aztecs called the turkey the *huehxolotl*. Native Americans called it an *omahksipi'kssii*. The scientific name, *meleagris gallopavo*, is a mash up of words that reference Greek mythology, roosters, and peacocks. Maybe we should just stick with *gobble, gobble*?

The **red flesh** that **hangs** over a turkey's **beak** is called a **snood**.

**Scientific Name:** Meleagris gallopavo
**Size:** Up to 50 inches long
**Habitat:** Woodlands near water in Europe, Asia, and the Americas
**Diet:** Seeds, insects, and small reptiles and amphibians

## Follow the Feathers

Next time you're on a nature walk, keep your eyes open for turkey feathers. Wild turkeys often leave their feathers behind after a scuffle. At first glance, the feathers may appear dull, but look closer, and you'll see they are iridescent.

Warm in a Fierce
Winter Storm,
Waiting...
Watching...

# Hunting for Prey

Foxes have long been admired for their keen hunting skills. A fox can hear a mouse stirring 25 feet away. The fox stalks its prey using all its senses, including a magnetic sense. It tiptoes on its paws, watches, waits, smells, and listens. When the fox hears a scamper that aligns with the magnetic field it's waiting for, it launches into the air and dives headfirst into the snow. Once the fox pins the mouse with its paws, it rips into its meal with its sharp teeth.

**Scientific Name:** Vulpes vulpes
**Size:** 35 to 40 inches long
**Habitat:** Everywhere from Arctic tundra to arid deserts around the world
**Diet:** Mice, rabbits, eggs, fruit, grain, and birds

Whenever they can, **foxes** hunt for **extra prey** and **bury** it until it's **needed**.

## Outfoxing Nature

What happens when you breed wild animals to feel less fear? Eventually, you domesticate them. Long ago, wolves evolved into dogs when they learned to no longer fear humans, keeping their smaller teeth and gentler wolf-pup features. Today, scientists are studying foxes to see how long it takes them to develop the friendly nature we love in dogs.

# Slick as a Seal

Like whales, dolphins, and otters, seals are underwater mammals. They appear to have evolved from an ancient line of weasel-like creatures that once lived on land. They still need air to breath, but they've adapted to life in the water in remarkable ways. Seals have layers of fat and fur to keep them warm. Their streamlined shape lets them race through the water. Wavy whiskers help them track currents produced as prey swim by. These delicate hairs are vital to hunting the nearly 20 pounds of food that seals eat each day.

## Seal Vision

Seals are helping scientists learn about parts of the oceans that have never been studied before. The seals wear sensors that map the ocean floor and record water temperature and salt levels. The data they send back reveal how the ocean is changing and where seals spend their time.

**Scientific Name:** Phoco vitulina
**Size:** 6 feet long
**Habitat:** Coastlines and lakes north of the equator
**Diet:** Fish, squid, and crustaceans

**Scientists** think **seals** are **color-blind**.

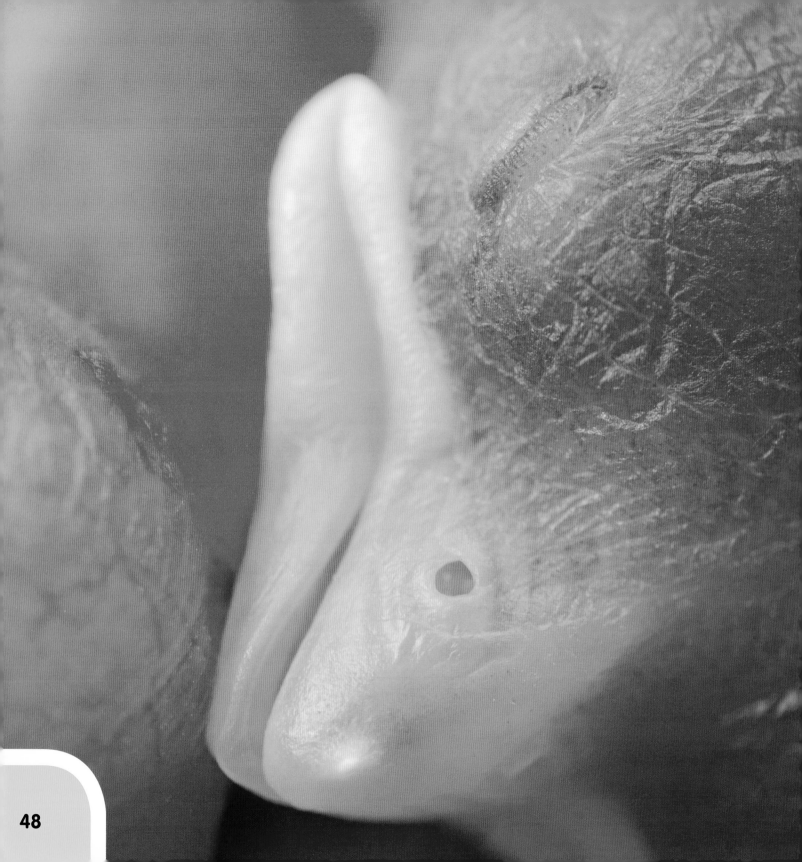

# From Egg to Lift Off

Inside the hard shell of an egg, a tiny chick has everything it needs to grow. The yolk feeds the young bird, and the shell protects it, while also allowing air through. When it's strong enough, the baby pecks through the shell. Hatchlings are often bald and helpless. Soon they'll grow fuzzy feathers and become nestlings. Older fledglings develop feathers and hop around on the ground. They're in training for the biggest adventure of their lives: flying!

**Oology** is the **study** of **eggs**. But so far **no one** has figured out "which came **first**, the **chicken** or the **egg**?"

## Designing a Nest

Birds use mud, twigs, spider webs, leaves, and moss to build their nests. Feathers add warmth and softness. Sparkly ribbons and other findings add bling!

# Whistle a Happy Tune

Orangutans love to play, wrestle, and even tickle each other. Hanging out with friends, laughing, and smiling evolved long before humans. Echoes of the *ha-ha* sounds we make when something strikes our funny bones can be heard in the *pant-pant* orangutans make during tickle fights. Sharing our playful nature works both ways—humans love teaching orangutans to whistle!

The **Apps for Apes** program lets **orangutans** use **iPads** to make zoo-to-zoo **video calls**, play Doodle Buddy with **friends**, and watch David Attenborough nature programs.

**Scientific Name:** Pongo pygmaeus
**Size:** 4 feet tall
**Habitat:** Rain forests in Sumatra and Borneo
**Diet:** Fruit, leaves, and very little meat

## Mwah!

It's always tricky to understand what animals are thinking and feeling—especially when their actions seem so familiar. Orangutans make a low squeaking sound by pushing their lips together, just like humans do when they kiss. But the orangutan version is more of a smack than a smooch. They use it to scare away predators.

# With Flying Colors

Having feathers is one of those things that makes a bird a bird. But there are almost as many different types of feathers as there are birds. They can range from fluffy wisps of down to stiff shafts that act almost like hands, helping birds steady themselves high in trees. Some feathers keep birds warm. Others help them fly. Often the most colorful feathers are used to attract female birds, although they may be even showier than we know. Birds can see more colors than humans can!

Making Waves

Good as Gold

**Like Butter**

**A Tropical Rainbow**

**Falling Water**

**Highly Hypnotic**

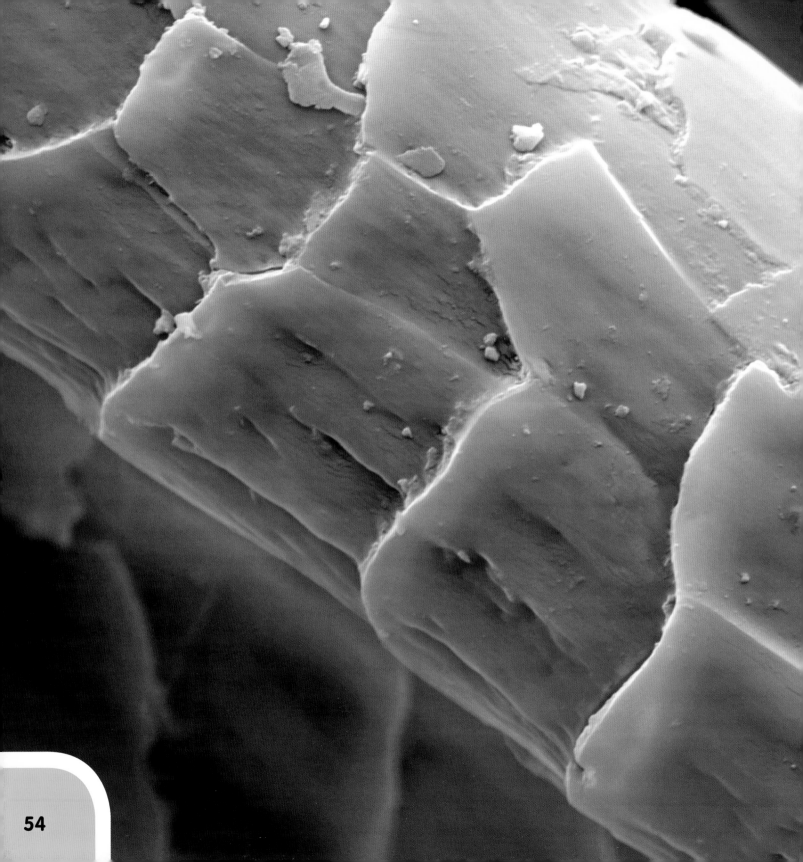

# An Icy Landscape?

# Fleece as White as Snow

Zooming in, in, in 2,500 times on a piece of wool reveals a textured tundra. Rabbits, goats, camels, and sheep all have wool coats. Although, it doesn't take a microscope to see freshly shorn wool is covered in fat and farm filth. But once it has been carefully washed and spun, it can be knit into warm sweaters and other comforting clothes.

**Scientific Name:** Ovis aries
**Size:** 4 feet
**Habitat:** Farms around the world
**Diet:** Grass and other plants

The **Vikings depended** on **sheep** for their **milk, meat,** and **hides.**

## A Four-Stomach Meal

Sheep eat a LOT of grass. And while that's totally healthy, it's not easy on the stomach. In fact, sheep need four stomach compartments to digest all that grass. Regurgitating the grass and chewing the cud makes what finally does make it down the hatch easier to absorb.

# The Brightest Bird

Their squawks and screeches may be mysterious to us, but one thing is clear: Macaws are highly intelligent birds. They test unfamiliar objects with their tongues, play with their feet, and spend hours hanging with friends in their flock. When faced with a puzzle, they can make surprising leaps in logic. And if they get the chance to listen to music, they even have favorite songs. Some scientists think parrots name their chicks just like humans do. One parrot could even understand the idea of zero, which gives new meaning to the phrase "bird brain."

**Scarlet macaws** don't just have **red** feathers. They **blush** when they get **excited**.

**Scientific Name:** Ara macao
**Size:** 30 inches long
**Habitat:** Rain forests, riverbanks, and grasslands in Mexico and Central and South America
**Diet:** Seeds, nuts, fruits, flowers, and leaves

## Bird Watching

If you're in the right place, it's easy to spot macaws in the sky. Their bright feathers help, but you'll also want to look for their slow wing beats and long tails trailing behind them. They often release long metallic calls as they fly.

# Sweet Dreams

Eat. Sleep. Repeat. That's the sloth motto. Relaxing in trees is a way of life for these gentle creatures. Their muscles are slack as hammocks, and they move like dreamy ballerinas. They spend long hours lounging on branches and eating leaves in slow motion. Even their insides move at a snail's pace, with some foods taking a month to be fully digested.

## Stranger than Fiction

Just 12,000 years ago, giant sloths roamed the Earth. They weighed in at 5 tons and had foot-long claws. The world is changing more quickly than it ever has before. Perhaps in another million years, all animals will have fur *and* feathers!

**Scientific Name:** Choloepus didactylus
**Size:** 20 to 30 inches long
**Habitat:** Tropical forests in Central and South America
**Diet:** Leaves, stems, buds, and fruit

Sloths **love** hibiscus **flowers** the way some **people** love **chocolate**.

# Behind the Lens

Now it's your turn! Grab a camera and start shooting whenever you see something that amazes you or makes you curious to learn more. If you want to go macro without spending too much money, snap a macro lens band over a cellphone camera. Whatever camera you use, these tips will help you get started.

The flash lights the subject.

The shutter acts like a camera, opening and closing to let light into the camera for short periods of time.

The lens is the curved piece of glass that light travels through before reaching a sensor or film inside the camera.

A tripod keeps the camera steady.

The size of the opening in the lens is the aperture. It's measured in fractions.

The focal point is the part of the image that's sharp.

The depth of field is the distance between the parts of an object that are in focus. In micro and macro photography, this distance is very small.

Some lenses have a short focal length and produce a wider angle of view. Other lenses have a longer focal length.

## Aperture Scale

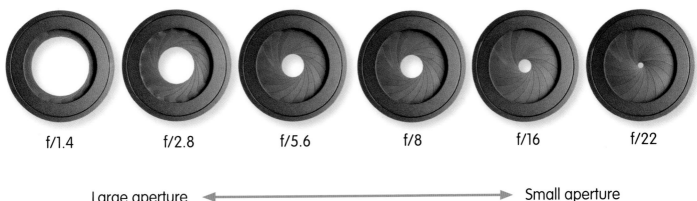

f/1.4     f/2.8     f/5.6     f/8     f/16     f/22

Large aperture  ⟵⟶  Small aperture
More light strikes image sensor  ⟵⟶  Less light strikes image sensor
Shallow Depth of Field (Focus)  ⟵⟶  Deep Depth of Field (Focus)

# Index